HOW TO ACHIEVE MENTAL WELLNESS

Strategies for Busy Professionals Thriving in a Demanding World

by Alex wells

TABLE OF CONTENTS

The value of mental health in today's stressful world

It is impossible to overestimate the significance of mental well-being in today's fast-paced and demanding world. Professionals in many different industries frequently encounter difficult situations that might have an impact on their mental health. The frequency of mental health problems among professionals must be acknowledged, as must the effects of poor mental health on productivity and general well-being.

The prevalence of mental health problems among professionals across all industries and levels of seniority is dangerously high. The stressful nature of work can play a role in the development of anxiety, depression, burnout, and other mental health issues, along with deadline pressures, high expectations, and the desire to consistently perform at a high level. The tensions and difficulties encountered in the workplace frequently provide an atmosphere conducive to the onset or worsening of these problems.

According to research, some professionals encounter mental health issues at some point in their working lives. The prevalence of such problems stresses the need for increased understanding and assistance and prioritizing mental well-being in the workplace.

Individual productivity and general well-being can both be severely impacted by poor mental health. Professionals may have trouble focusing, making decisions, or sustaining good relationships when their mental health is damaged. Stress, anxiety, or overwhelming sensations take over the mind, which can seriously reduce working effectiveness and productivity.

Furthermore, the implications of poor mental well-being go beyond performance at work. The ability to experience joy, happiness, and fulfillment in one's personal life is also influenced by mental health. Increased irritation, decreased emotional availability, and a lack of excitement or energy can all have a negative impact on relationships. Additionally, a lack of mental well-being can have physical consequences, including weakened immunity, greater susceptibility to disease, and a higher chance of developing chronic health disorders.

Understanding how poor mental health affects professional productivity and general well-being makes it obvious that mental health should be prioritized. A person's career will gain by investing in their mental health, but they will also lead more rewarding lives.

The significance of addressing mental health concerns is supported by knowledge of the pervasiveness of mental health problems among professionals and the wide-ranging effects of poor mental well-being. To help busy professionals prioritize and attain mental well-being amid a demanding environment, we will cover practical ideas and approaches as we go further into this book.

Busy professionals are the target audience

This book was created with busy professionals in mind who frequently have to deal with demanding and difficult work environments. It is critical to understand the particular pressures and time limits this target audience has and the special obstacles individuals confront in preserving their mental well-being.

Describe the difficulties busy professionals face in preserving their mental health.

Busy professionals face various difficulties that may be barriers to their mental health. These difficulties might include:

High workload: Busy professionals frequently deal with overwhelming workloads and strict deadlines, which leaves them with little time for leisure or self-care.

Time pressure: Time restrictions and the need to achieve strict deadlines can put enormous pressure on professionals, making them anxious and overwhelmed.

Work-life imbalance: Striking a balance between work and personal life can be difficult for professionals who spend a lot of time on their professions and little time with their families, friends, or taking care of themselves.

High expectations: Professionals are frequently held to a high standard and expected to perform extraordinarily well.

Ongoing education and development: Many professionals work in fast-paced fields that need ongoing education and adaptation, adding to the pressure of remaining current and competitive.

Call attention to the particular pressures and time restraints they face.

Professional tasks and obligations present unique challenges to busy professionals. These stressors might consist of:

Demands from clients or stakeholders: Professionals frequently have to handle client or stakeholder expectations and demands, which can add to their stress and workload.

Pressures associated with career progress: The desire for professional growth and promotion can raise stress levels and intensify competitiveness.

Travel and mobility needs: Working people who regularly travel or need to be mobile may need to help maintaining a healthy work-life balance and regular self-care routines.

Decision-making responsibilities: Professionals frequently have to make important decisions that might negatively influence their businesses, which adds to their stress and causes decision fatigue.

Leadership and management responsibilities: Professionals in leadership or management roles may have particular pressures connected to managing disagreements, directing teams, and achieving corporate goals.

Understanding these particular pressures and time restraints enables us to customize the tactics and approaches offered in this book to the unique requirements of busy professionals, assuring their applicability and efficacy.

Overview of the book's goals and organization

Despite their demanding work circumstances, this book is a comprehensive manual to assist time-pressed professionals in achieving and maintaining maximum mental well-being. It offers a well-organized framework of tactics, knowledge, and tools to help professionals improve mental health and well-being.

The chapters in the book cover a variety of topics related to mental wellness, such as understanding mental wellness, evaluating current mental health, laying a foundation for mental wellness, managing stress and overwhelm, developing coping mechanisms, fostering work-life balance, enhancing productivity and focus, cultivating positive mental health habits, seeking professional help when necessary, and maintaining mental wellness over the long term.

Each chapter goes deep into a particular subject, offers helpful advice and suggestions, and suggests doable actions that busy professionals may use daily. Busy professionals will have the information and resources required to prioritize their mental well-being and succeed in their demanding world by adhering to the advice provided in this book.

Give a concise synopsis of the techniques and subjects addressed in the book.

This book seeks to give busy professionals who want to attain and maintain excellent mental well-being in a demanding environment a complete arsenal. It includes a wide range of tactics and subjects that are especially suited to the special difficulties that professionals experience in their working life. Here is a quick rundown of the main techniques and subjects you may anticipate learning about:

Understanding mental wellness: Gain a greater grasp of mental wellness, its components, and the significance of sustaining a good mental state.

Evaluating present mental health: Take a self-assessment to gauge your current mental health, pinpoint any possible problem areas, and monitor your development.

Laying a solid foundation for mental well-being: Develop good habits and routines, such as self-awareness, mindfulness, and physical health, that promote your mental wellness.

Managing stress and overwhelm: Develop time management abilities, boundary-setting methods, and stress reduction techniques to reduce stress and avoid burnout.

Developing coping mechanisms: Finding healthy and helpful coping skills can help you overcome obstacles, develop emotional fortitude, and ask for help when needed.

Promoting work-life harmony: Look into methods to achieve a harmonic balance between work and personal life, enabling fulfilling leisure activities.

Increasing productivity and attention: Acquire skills to sharpen focus, control distractions, and increase productivity to get more done while preserving your mental health.

Developing good mental health habits: For long-term mental well-being, use self-care, gratitude, optimism, and resilience-building exercises.

Seeking professional assistance when necessary: Recognize the warning signals that call for assistance from a professional, look into mental health resources, and understand how to start dialogues about mental health without stigma.

Long-term mental wellness maintenance: For continued well-being, create a tailored long-term mental wellness strategy, overcome challenges, and value lifelong learning and personal development.

Establish goals for the reader's journey to mental well-being.

As a busy professional, it takes effort, self-reflection, and a willingness to make positive adjustments to start along this path to mental well-being. You'll discover useful advice, doable actions, and examples from real life throughout this book to help you improve.

There is no one-size-fits-all answer, but the concepts and approaches in this book may be customized to your unique requirements and situations. Expect to understand your mental health better, acquire useful techniques for handling stress and overcoming obstacles, and create a positive outlook on life.

It's crucial to remember that obtaining mental wellness is a continuous process, and this book is a great tool to help you along the way. You may improve your mental toughness, find more fulfillment in both your career and personal life, and ultimately flourish in the challenging environment by putting the ideas and approaches taught into practice.

Together, let's start along this transforming path to mental wellness, giving you the tools, you need to live a happier, more balanced life as a busy professional.

UNDERSTANDING MENTAL WELLNESS

An explanation of mental health and its components

We will examine the idea of mental well-being in this chapter and some of its key elements. Beyond just being free from mental disease, mental wellness refers to a condition of health that includes our emotional, psychological, and social well-being.

Talk about how mental well-being is a comprehensive concept that includes social, psychological, and emotional well-being.

Mental wellness is a comprehensive approach that considers the interwoven components of our life and is not only about our emotions or ideas. Understanding and effectively controlling our emotions, building wholesome relationships, and engaging in self-care are all important components of emotional well-being. Our capacity to overcome obstacles, have a positive outlook and develop resilience are all parts of psychological well-being. Social well-being is our capacity to create and sustain meaningful connections, participate in positive social interactions, and give back to our communities.

Let's consider Sarah's narrative to show how mental well-being is a comprehensive concept. Successful executive Sarah works in a demanding corporate environment. Despite her success professionally, she still struggles with anxiety, loneliness, and a lack of contentment. She understands that her emotional well-being is harmed because she disregards her needs and has no support network. She becomes aware of the value of protecting her mental well-being by self-reflection, seeking assistance, prioritizing self-care, going to therapy, and establishing a solid social support system. Sarah improves her general mental well-being as she starts to focus on her emotional well-being, which brings about a feeling of balance and contentment in her life.

Recognizing the interconnectedness and equal importance of each component helps us appreciate the holistic nature of mental well-being. One part might affect the others if neglected, compromising our mental health. We may live more fully, satisfactorily, and resiliently by caring for our emotional, psychological, and social well-being.

Describe the significance of harmony and balance in all spheres of life.

Finding harmony and balance in all aspects of our lives is necessary to achieve mental well-being. It entails coordinating everyday activities and decisions with our beliefs, objectives, and priorities. We could feel stressed, overwhelmed, or disconnected when there is a lack of balance.

Think about Mark, a motivated professional who spends most of his time working. He has poor connections with family members, rarely participates in leisure activities, and neglects his physical health. Mark is conscious of how his lack of equilibrium harms his mental health. Through introspection and encouragement, he understands the need to incorporate self-care practices into his daily routine, establish boundaries to safeguard his private time, and foster connections. Mark is happier, his relationships improve, and he has a newfound sense of purpose as he begins to value harmony and balance in his life.

Recognizing that our mental health is not primarily based on our success or accomplishments in the workplace is the first step toward finding balance. Setting limits, prioritizing self-care, and achieving a healthy balance between work and personal life, as well as other areas like hobbies, relationships, and personal development, are all part of it. We may encourage mental well-being and feel more fulfilled overall by nourishing each element of our lives and working toward balance.

The first step to developing and sustaining good mental well-being is to understand mental health as a holistic concept and appreciate the value of balance and harmony in all facets of life. We can witness the transformational potential of treating our emotional, psychological, and social well-being and aiming for balance via tales like Sarah's and Mark's. We will investigate viable tactics and methods to foster mental wellness, incorporate them into our everyday lives, and establish a harmonic equilibrium that supports our general well-being.

Examining how stress affects mental health

We will examine the profound effect of stress on our mental health in this part. Long-term stress can have several physiological and psychological impacts and is strongly associated with the onset or worsening of prevalent mental health problems, including anxiety and depression.

Describe the physical and mental implications of persistent stress.

Chronic stress may significantly negatively impact our body and mind since it refers to prolonged exposure to stimuli without receiving enough respite. Chronic stress physiologically causes the release of stress hormones like cortisol, which, when continuously high, can affect several biological systems. This interference may result in the following:

Impairment of immune function: Long-term stress compromises immunity, leaving us more vulnerable to infections and diseases.

Enhanced risk of cardiovascular issues: Long-term stress raises blood pressure and increases the risk of heart disease and other cardiovascular conditions.

Digestive issues: Stress can affect food absorption, resulting in gastrointestinal disorders, including irritable bowel syndrome (IBS) and acid reflux.

Sleep disturbances: Prolonged stress can interrupt sleep cycles and cause insomnia, negatively affecting mental and physical health.

Chronic stress has a psychologically substantial negative effect on our mental health. It may result in:

Heightened anxiety: Chronic stress can make people feel more anxious, uneasy, and restless, leading to the emergence or worsening of anxiety disorders.

Mood disturbances: Prolonged stress can increase the risk of mood disorders, including depression and cause irritability, mood swings, and other behavioral problems.

Cognitive problems: Prolonged stress may impede memory, focus, and decision-making skills, affecting cognitive function.

An understanding of the physiological and psychological impacts of chronic stress emphasizes the need to manage stress to preserve mental well-being appropriately.

Discuss the connection between stress and prevalent mental health issues, including anxiety and depression.

Anxiety and depression are two mental health problems that frequently coexist with stress. These disorders may be triggered or made worse by chronic stress. Following are some explanations of how stress and mental health are related:

Anxiety: Increased anxiety levels can cause excessive worrying, unfounded concerns, and panic attacks as a result of chronic stress. Long-term stress exposure can overwhelm the body and mind, which can lead to the emergence of anxiety disorders.

Depression: Long-term stress raises the possibility of developing or exacerbating depression. Energy levels might be depleted, motivation can be reduced, and mood can be badly impacted by the ongoing pressure and emotional toll of stress, eventually leading to a low condition.

It's significant to remember that each person's response to stress is unique, and not everyone who suffers from stress will experience anxiety or despair. However, understanding the connection between stress and these widespread mental health issues emphasizes the need to manage stress to delay the development or reduce symptoms.

We gain insight into the significance of stress management in promoting and sustaining mental well-being by studying the physiological and psychological impacts of chronic stress and its relationship to mental health disorders. In the following chapters, we will examine useful tactics and methods for managing stress, minimizing its effects on mental health, and promoting a sense of well-being despite the demands of our busy lives.

Identifying the symptoms of poor mental health

This part will examine the warning signs and symptoms of poor mental well-being. It is essential to be aware of these signs since they may be used as a starting point to determine whether our mental health may be in danger. We may recognize our indications of distress and make proactive efforts toward getting help and enhancing our mental well-being by promoting self-reflection and self-awareness.

Provide a thorough list of the symptoms and indications of poor mental health.

Awareness of the warning signs and symptoms of poor mental well-being can be helpful when our mental health requires care. While every person's experience will be different, the following are some typical signs that imply poor mental health:

    a.   Ongoing emotions of melancholy, emptiness, or hopelessness
    b.   A rise in agitation or fury
    c.   Withdrawal from relationships or social activities
    d.   A considerable rise or reduction in appetite or weight
    e.   f. sleep disorders such as insomnia or oversleeping

f.   f. Tiredness or a lack of energy

g.   g. Having trouble focusing or making judgments

h.   Loss of enjoyment or interest in once-enjoyed activities

i.   Physical signs such as headaches, tense muscles, or intestinal issues

j.   j. A greater reliance on drugs and alcohol as a coping mechanism

k.   k. Constant worrying or racing thoughts

l.   l. Guilt, a sense of being unworthy, or severe self-criticism

m.   m. Recurrent suicidal or dead thoughts

It's crucial to remember that while exhibiting any of these symptoms might be a warning sign for possible discomfort, they do not always signify a mental health condition. It may be helpful to seek professional care from a mental health specialist if you or someone you know consistently exhibit multiple symptoms.

Promote introspection and self-awareness to spot your indications of stress.

Self-reflection and self-awareness are essential for identifying one's distress symptoms. There may be particular signs specific to each person that indicate their mental health is at risk. By practicing self-awareness, we may more easily recognize when anything seems odd or out of balance inside of us.

It's important to routinely check in with ourselves if we want to promote self-reflection. You might find it useful to inquire about the following:

a.   How do I feel on a personal level? Do I have any lingering bad feelings or mood swings?

b.   How am I feeling physically? Do I have any signs of stress or mental exhaustion in my body?

c.   Do I tend to think negatively or critically of myself?

d.   How are my social contacts and relationships? Am I retreating from family members or feeling distant from them?

e. Have my sleep habits, appetite, or general energy level changed significantly?

We develop a heightened awareness of our distress signals by deliberately practicing self-reflection and self-awareness. Because of our increased self-awareness, we are more equipped to seek help, practice self-care, and make the necessary adjustments to enhance our mental well-being.

We can better identify when our mental health requires care when we are aware of the symptoms of poor mental well-being and encourage self-reflection. As we read this book, we will examine methods and tactics to treat these symptoms and develop our general mental health. Remember that maintaining our mental health is a lifelong effort that calls for awareness and self-compassion.

ASSESSING YOUR CURRENT MENTAL WELLNESS

Conducting a mental health self-evaluation

This chapter focuses on how to do a thorough self-evaluation of your present mental well-being. A mental health assessment offers insightful information about your well-being, reveals your strengths, and draws attention to areas needing improvement. You will better understand your mental well-being and set the foundation for personal development and progress via tools, quizzes, and guided self-reflection.

Offer readers tools and quizzes to assess their mental well-being.

This book offers several tools and quizzes to encourage self-reflection and examination to help you measure your mental well-being. These resources are made to assist you in recognizing and considering many facets of your mental health, such as:

Emotional stability: Evaluating your emotional condition, spotting trends in mood swings, and investigating the variety and intensity of your feelings.

Mindfulness of the mind: examining your mental health to see if your thinking patterns, self-talk, and cognitive processes are helpful or harmful.

Financial security: evaluating your social network's support, relationships' caliber, and social connections.

Adaptive strategies: evaluate the efficiency of your present coping mechanisms for dealing with stress, adversity, and obstacles.

Self-care techniques: Identifying your self-care practices and determining whether they sufficiently address your physical, mental, and emotional needs.

Using these tools and surveys, you will learn important things about your mental health and have a better knowledge of areas that may need attention and development.

Lead readers through a self-reflection and assessment process

This book will lead you through a process of self-reflection and evaluation in addition to the tools and quizzes. Introspection, openness, and a desire to examine your ideas, feelings, and behaviors are all necessary for self-reflection. You will be prompted to consider several facets of your mental well-being through guided activities and suggestions, such as:

Recognizing stresses: Understanding the effects of stress on your mental health and identifying its causes.

Patterns and triggers: discovering reoccurring patterns and triggers in your thoughts, feelings, and actions to improve your mental health.

Resources and Strengths: Identify your assets, networks of support, and internal resources that may be used to improve your mental health.

Potential for development: Decide on areas you want to work on and improve for greater mental health.

The self-reflection and evaluation process makes understanding your present mental well-being possible. It promotes self-awareness, supports personal development, and gives you the tools to take charge of your mental health.

You may learn a lot about your mental health by doing some self-assessment, using the supplied tools and questionnaires, and actively participating in self-reflection. With this information, you may advance in improving your mental health, better understanding your present situation and the issues you want to address.

Recognizing individual stresses and triggers

In this section, we'll concentrate on assisting you in pinpointing particular stresses and triggers that have a detrimental effect on your mental health. By identifying these issues, you may have more control over your mental health and create plans to deal with or lessen their impact.

Assist readers in identifying certain stresses and triggers that harm their mental well-being.

Knowing what affects your mental health is the first step in identifying personal triggers and stresses. Each person may experience several triggers that have a varied effect on their mental health. You can take proactive steps to lessen their harmful effects by being aware of these triggers. Consider the following factors while assessing your triggers and stressors:

Stressors at work: Think about the workplace elements or duties that cause stress. A heavy workload, strict deadlines, confrontations with coworkers, or a lack of control over your job are all possible causes.

Stressors in one's own life: Examine the difficulties or stresses you face in your personal life, such as marital issues, money worries, family obligations, or significant life transitions.

Environmental catalysts: Think about the outside influences in your environment that cause stress or impact your mental health, such as loudness, clutter, or a lack of privacy.

Social triggers: Think about the dynamics of your relationships and social interactions. Exist any particular people or social circumstances that always make you feel stressed or uneasy? Conflicts, unhealthy relationships, or pressure from the outside world might be the cause.

Personal stressors: Examine your mental habits and any expectations or demands placed on you. Are you stressed by perfectionistic impulses, arbitrary standards, or negative self-talk?

You may learn more about the stresses and triggers that affect your mental health most by investigating these areas.

Offer techniques for limiting or controlling these triggers.

Develop techniques to control or lessen their impacts once you have recognized your unique triggers and stresses. Here are some ideas to take into account:

Stress reduction methods: Learn and practice several stress-management approaches, such as deep breathing exercises, mindfulness meditation, exercise, or taking part in relaxing hobbies.

Set limits and control your time: To stop excessive stress from affecting your personal life, establish clear boundaries between your professional and personal lives. To prevent feeling overloaded, prioritize activities, delegate when you can, and use good time management techniques.

Communicating and being assertive: Improve your ability to communicate so that you can express your wants, establish limits, and ask for help when you need it. Interpersonal tension and disputes can be lessened through effective communication.

Self-care techniques: Implement routine self-care practices geared at your physical, mental, and emotional well-being. This may entail doing things you like, cultivating self-compassion, making time for relaxation, and prioritizing sleep and a nutritious diet.

Reframing and problem-solving: Hone your problem-solving abilities to deal with certain pressures or triggers. To lessen the effect of negative ideas on your mental well-being, find alternate viewpoints or rephrase them.

Seek assistance: For help and direction, speak with close friends, relatives, or experts you trust. Having a support network may offer invaluable insight, counsel, and emotional support in trying circumstances.

Keep in mind that coping with triggers and stresses is a lifelong effort. Trying out various tactics and customizing them to your needs is crucial because something other than what works for one individual might not work for another.

You may dramatically lessen the detrimental effects of your own triggers and stressors on your mental well-being by identifying them and putting effective management measures into place. With this increased awareness and proactive attitude, you'll be better equipped to handle difficult circumstances with fortitude and take action to maintain a healthier mental state.

Considering how mental health affects career success

This part will examine how mental health and career performance relate. By thinking about this link, you better comprehend the beneficial effects that enhancing your mental well-being can have on your work and your professional life.

Examine the link between psychological well-being and career success.

Mental health and career performance, there is a significant association. Your job may be significantly impacted in several ways when your mental health is disturbed. When studying this link, bear in mind the following important factors:

Performance and productivity: Your performance and productivity at work are greatly influenced by your mental health. The ability to think, make wise judgments, and sustain attention and concentration are all enhanced by good mental health. On the other hand, poor mental health can result in lower performance, difficulties managing tasks, and reduced productivity.

Creativity and problem-solving skills: Your ability to think critically and be creative is improved by mental well-being. Positive mental health increases your resilience, creativity, and imaginative problem-solving capacity. Conversely, if your mental health is impaired, you can have cognitive problems and find it hard to develop fresh ideas or answers.

Relationships with people: To succeed professionally, one must establish and maintain good connections with clients, supervisors, and coworkers. Mental well-being is important in terms of how you relate to and communicate with other people. Strong relationships, successful teamwork, and constructive dispute resolution are all possible when you are mentally well. Conversely, poor mental health can cause problems with interpersonal connections, lack of collaboration, and communication problems.

Job satisfaction and advancement: Career satisfaction and advancement are intimately related to mental well-being. When your mental health is in good shape, you are more likely to find work satisfying, have a sense of purpose, and be motivated to explore possibilities for professional progress. On the other hand, having bad mental health might result in unhappiness, fatigue, and a lack of ambition to grow in your profession.

Inspire readers to think about the beneficial effects of enhancing their mental well-being on their careers.

Your job may benefit significantly if you improve your mental health. Your mental health can be a priority if you:

To improve performance and productivity: Your performance and productivity at work can increase if you take action to improve your mental well-being. You may maximize your cognitive capacities, retain attention, and boost your overall productivity by controlling stress, developing a positive outlook, and engaging in self-care.

Develop wholesome connections: You can create and maintain healthy connections at work when you put your mental health first. A peaceful workplace, greater cooperation, and enhanced collaboration are all benefits of improved communication, emotional health, and interpersonal skills.

Encourage adaptation and resilience: Investing in your mental well-being may increase your resilience and flexibility and better deal with difficulties and changes in your professional environment. You can overcome losses, take lessons from mistakes, and seize fresh possibilities if you have the emotional and psychological capacity.

Boosting contentment and happiness in the workplace: Greater professional happiness and fulfillment can result from putting your mental health first. You may discover fulfillment and purpose in your professional pursuits by coordinating your values, establishing sound boundaries, and promoting work-life balance.

Encourage long-term professional growth: It is possible to seek personal and professional progress as long as you maintain your mental health. The ability to learn, develop new abilities, and seize opportunities for job growth increases when you keep an optimistic outlook.

It inspires one to prioritize one's well-being to get readers to think about how enhancing their mental well-being might benefit one's work. You may start your road toward leading a happier and happier work life by realizing the connection between mental health and career success.

BUILDING A FOUNDATION FOR MENTAL WELLNESS

Developing mindfulness and self-awareness

In this chapter, we will discuss the significance of developing self-awareness and mindfulness as a basis for mental well-being. Giving them methods to control stress, improve attention, and advance general well-being will greatly assist busy professionals.

Explain mindfulness techniques to working professionals

The practice of mindfulness entails consciously focusing on the present moment without passing judgment. It promotes greater clarity and awareness by allowing us to interact with our experiences, thoughts, and emotions completely. Introducing mindfulness techniques to busy professionals can make it easier for them to balance their personal and professional life demands.

Imagine, for instance, that busy executive Emma is confronted with several deadlines, and a demanding work environment burdens her. Emma may bring her focus back to the present now, relieve tension, and enhance her ability to prioritize activities by incorporating mindfulness into her daily routine, such as taking brief breaks for focused breathing exercises or practicing mindful eating over lunch. Thanks to these mindfulness exercises, she can eventually approach problems with a more composed and relaxed attitude.

Stress the advantages of self-awareness in reducing stress and enhancing mental health.

A fundamental ability that enables us to identify and comprehend our thoughts, feelings, and behaviors is self-awareness. Busy workers may enhance their mental wellness and stress management skills by being more self-aware of their stress triggers, emotions, and reaction patterns.

Think about James, an aspirational entrepreneur. James frequently noticed that he was easily upset and stressed, which harmed his relationships with his team members and reduced his productivity. James became aware of the link between his high standards, perfectionism, and stress levels as a result of self-reflection and the development of self-awareness. James put tactics like establishing reasonable objectives, using stress-reduction techniques, and getting help from a mentor or coach into action by understanding these tendencies and adopting self-compassion. As a result, James had better connections at work, better emotional health, and more productivity.

Stress management and fostering mental well-being are two things that may be managed and promoted by busy professionals by emphasizing the advantages of self-awareness.

The lives of busy professionals can be improved by using mindfulness techniques and developing self-awareness. These techniques can help you stay grounded despite the chaos, sharpen your attention and focus, and increase your general well-being. This chapter will provide busy professionals with the tools to lay a strong foundation for their mental well-being via self-reflection, guided mindfulness exercises, and good practices.

Developing healthy behaviors to improve your physical health

The vital function that physical well-being plays in fostering mental wellness will be discussed in this chapter. This article discuss how developing good physical and mental health habits may help a busy professional. We'll also offer helpful advice for keeping a healthy lifestyle despite a busy schedule.

Examine how physical health affects mental health.

There are many connections between physical and mental health. It has a direct good effect on our mental health when we give our physical health priority. These are some important ideas to bear in mind:

Reduction of stress: Endorphins are naturally occurring mood enhancers released during regular physical activity like exercise or movement. A more balanced mental state results from exercise because it lowers stress hormones and encourages relaxation.

Better mental performance: Blood flow to the brain is increased by exercise, which improves concentration, memory, and cognitive ability. It encourages the development of new neurons, which benefits how well we can reason, solve problems, and make choices.

Vibrance and energy: To manage the demands of a hectic work life, we need the energy and vigor to care for our physical health through a balanced diet, enough sleep, and frequent exercise. Improvements in productivity and a stronger sense of well-being are related to higher energy levels.

Managing one's emotions: A healthy lifestyle and physical activity can favorably influence our ability to regulate our emotions, allowing us better to control our stress, anxiety, and mood swings. It helps people become more emotionally resilient and offers a natural release for suppressed feelings.

Busy professionals may prioritize their physical health as a fundamental element of preserving total mental wellness by realizing the connection between physical and mental wellness.

Offer helpful advice for continuing to live a healthy lifestyle despite a hectic schedule.

Even though it might be difficult for working professionals to maintain a healthy lifestyle, it is essential for promoting mental wellness. The following are some helpful pointers for creating wholesome habits:

Place a high priority on exercise: Even in modest doses, include movement or exercise into your daily schedule. You may schedule quick walks during breaks, choose the stairs over the elevator, or discover a regular physical activity that you love.

Eat conscientiously: Put balanced nutrition first and make informed eating decisions. Plan and prepare nutritious meals in advance to reduce your reliance on processed or unhealthy foods. Meals should be enjoyed slowly, and portion quantities should be considered.

Make sure you get enough rest: Make it a point to have a regular sleeping schedule that enables you to obtain enough good sleep. Establish a wind-down ritual, make your environment sleep-friendly, and limit your time with electronics before bed.

Reduce tension by using relaxation methods: Include relaxation methods like breathing exercises, meditation, or mindfulness practices in your everyday routine. Even a short period of relaxation can lower stress levels and improve mental health.

Establish boundaries and give self-care a priority: Decide on boundaries between your personal and professional lives so that you may schedule self-care activities. Spend time with loved ones, indulge in hobbies, or express your creativity—whatever brings you joy, relaxation, and fulfillment—should be given priority.

Find responsibility and support: Participate in a support system or think about teaming up with a wellness buddy who can keep you accountable and inspired to maintain a healthy lifestyle. A person with similar objectives might be a family member, friend, or coworker.

By putting these useful suggestions into practice, busy professionals may gradually develop good physical wellness habits, which in turn help to promote improved mental wellness. Professionals must balance their physical health and work-related responsibilities to succeed in their demanding positions and preserve their overall well-being. Doing so builds resilience, energy, and a positive outlook.

Remember, you may significantly enhance your physical and emotional wellness by making tiny adjustments and continuing your efforts. By prioritizing your physical health, you build a solid foundation for your mental wellbeing and establish the parameters for long-term achievement and enjoyment in both your personal and professional life.

Fostering an atmosphere that is supportive of mental health

This chapter will discuss the value of having a strong social support system for preserving mental health. We'll talk about establishing connections and asking friends, family, and coworkers for help to maintain a positive atmosphere promoting mental health.

Stress the value of having a supportive network for preserving mental health.

A strong social support system is essential for preserving mental health. A support system of people understanding, empathizing with, and encouraging us may positively influence our general well-being. This is why having a strong support system is crucial:

Emotional assistance: In difficult circumstances, a support network provides a secure place to vent feelings, voice worries, and get advice. Emotional support increases emotional resiliency, reduces feelings of loneliness, and offers affirmation.

Confirmation and viewpoint: We can feel validated and reassured by interacting with people who share our experiences and can sympathize with them. It enables us to observe things from several aspects and gives us perspective on our struggles, which improves our ability to solve problems and make decisions.

Stress management: Being a member of a supportive network helps lower stress levels by providing a feeling of community, opportunities for social interaction, and a place to talk about and process stress. Gaining support and having meaningful interactions can boost emotions of calm and well-being.

Motivation and accountability: A supporting network may hold us responsible for our objectives and commitments. They may provide words of support, inspiration, and constructive criticism, which helps keep us concentrated on the path to mental well-being.

Provide pointers on establishing connections and looking for assistance from coworkers, friends, and family

The first step in developing a supportive environment for mental well-being is establishing relationships and asking friends, family, and coworkers for help. Here are some tips to encourage these connections:

Encourage open dialogue: Encourage honest and open communication with coworkers, friends, and family. Encourage open communication of ideas, emotions, and worries. When someone reaches out, actively listen to them and assist.

Increase vulnerability and trust: Be dependable, trustworthy, and respectful of secrecy to build trust. By expressing your feelings and experiences, you can encourage others to be vulnerable.

Look for others with similar views: Be in the company of people who value their mental health and well-being. Find groups or friends with similar beliefs and objectives that support you. Join groups or activities that reflect your interests and ideals.

Make use of the resources at hand: Investigate employee assistance programs, counseling services, and organizational initiatives that support mental well-being. Utilize expert services, such as therapists or coaches, who may offer direction and support.

Use proactive support: Actively assist others in your network by lending a sympathetic ear, demonstrating empathy, and delivering words of encouragement. Keep an eye out for their welfare and lend a hand if necessary. Small acts of generosity and support may have a big impact.

Give self-care in relationships top priority: You may encourage self-care by talking about and exchanging well-being techniques with your network. Plan mental well-being-promoting activities like team-building events, meditation sessions, or wellness workshops.

You may establish a supportive atmosphere that promotes mental well-being by actively forming relationships and asking for help from friends, family, and coworkers. It's important to remember that creating these connections takes time and work, but the rewards for your mental health are immense. Your road to preserving and improving your mental well-being may be built on a foundation of strength, resilience, and progress if you have the support and understanding of others.

STRATEGIES FOR MANAGING STRESS AND OVERWHELM

Strategies for reducing stress

In this chapter, we'll look at practical stress-reduction methods that can assist working professionals in managing their stress and overload. Practical methods for controlling stress in daily life may be obtained by introducing deep breathing exercises, meditation, and relaxation techniques.

Explain stress-reduction practices such as deep breathing exercises, meditation, and relaxation methods

Techniques for managing stress are useful tools for bringing about mental well-being and lowering stress levels. Effective practices that may be included in a busy professional's routine include deep breathing exercises, meditation, and relaxation techniques. An overview of each tactic is provided below:

Exercises for deep breathing: Deep breathing takes long, slow breaths to trigger the body's relaxation response. Increased oxygen flow, a sensation of serenity, and stress reduction are all benefits. Exercises that include guided deep breathing may be done anywhere, anytime, and they quickly reduce tension.

Meditation: To attain mental clarity and relaxation during meditation, you must concentrate and quiet your mind. It may be performed using various methods, including mindfulness meditation, loving-kindness meditation, or visualization. Regular meditation can lower stress, increase focus, and improve general well-being.

Relaxation methods: Exercises that promote relaxation and ease tension in the body include progressive muscle relaxation, guided visualization, and listening to calming music. These strategies can be very beneficial when treating physical signs of stress like muscular tightness or headaches.

Offer detailed guidance for integrating these methods into a busy professional's daily schedule.

Step-by-step instructions may be offered to help active professionals incorporate these stress management practices into their everyday schedules. Consider this:

Exercises for deep breathing: Describe a basic deep breathing technique that may be done when there are only brief breaks or a lot of tension. Give directions on taking a deep breath in through the nose, holding it for a while, and then releasing gently through the mouth while stressing how important it is to concentrate on the breath and put aside distracting thoughts.

Meditation: Give advice on how to begin meditating, including where to find a quiet area, how to arrange a certain time, and how to start with brief sessions. Inform listeners how to concentrate on their breathing, acknowledge their thoughts without passing judgment, and gently bring their attention back to the present.

Relaxation methods: Explain progressive muscle relaxation by sequentially tensing and relaxing various muscle groups. Include a step-by-step procedure that motivates people to concentrate on each muscle group and relieve tension gradually.

By offering detailed instructions, busy professionals may quickly incorporate these stress-reduction methods into their regular schedules, enhancing mental well-being and lowering feelings of overwhelm.

In the following parts, we'll continue to discuss various methods for dealing with stress and overwhelm, such as time management and prioritizing techniques, boundary-setting, and saying "no" without feeling bad. These techniques will provide active individuals with the tools to manage heavy workloads while preserving their mental health.

Capacity for prioritizing tasks and managing time

This section will discuss managing your time well to avoid feeling overwhelmed. To better manage their workload and maintain their mental health, readers will learn how to prioritize projects and assign duties as appropriate.

To prevent feeling overwhelmed, provide helpful tips on time management.

Effective time management is crucial for busy professionals to feel in control of their workload and reduce stress. Here are some useful pointers to aid with time management:

Prioritize tasks: Determine the most crucial and urgent jobs that require immediate attention first. To-do lists and task management applications are useful tools for organizing and prioritizing things according to their due dates and priority.

Break things down into manageable steps: Big projects or jobs might be intimidating. To prevent feeling intimidated, divide things into more manageable chunks. Completing one step at a time can help you feel like you're making progress and have accomplished something.

Create deadlines and realistic goals: Set deadlines and reasonable goals for each assignment. Be aware of your limitations and refrain from over-committing. Setting realistic objectives can decrease your risk of feeling overloaded and will boost your drive and happiness when you achieve them.

Utilize time-blocking strategies: Establish time slots for various jobs or activities. Make a timetable allowing certain periods for concentrated work, breaks, meetings, and personal pursuits. This aids in structuring work and encouraging productivity.

Eschew multitasking: The effectiveness of multitasking and stress levels may suffer. Instead, concentrate and give each work your full attention. This increases focus and increases the caliber of the task.

Reduce distractions: Determine and eliminate any distractions that could occur, such as email notifications, social media, or interruptions from coworkers. Create a setting at work that encourages concentration and engagement.

Show readers how to assign duties as required and prioritize work.

For efficient time management and to lessen overwhelm, it's important to prioritize work and know when to delegate. Here are some tips on how to prioritize and assign tasks efficiently:

Analyze the importance and urgency of the task: Determine the priority and urgency of your responsibilities. While significant activities support long-term goals, urgent tasks demand immediate attention. Set urgent and vital tasks in order of importance.

Think about your assets and strengths: Determine which duties best fit your skills and areas of experience. Give others the responsibility for things they can handle well, or don't demand your direct involvement. Not only does delegating responsibilities reduce your workload, but it also allows others to offer their abilities.

Communicate and work together: With coworkers, managers, or team members, express task priorities and deadlines clearly. Work with others to maximize output and establish a shared knowledge of obligations. Stress is decreased, and misconceptions are avoided with effective communication.

Assess workload capability: Assess your workload and capability regularly. Consider talking to your manager or other team members about possible solutions, such as transferring jobs or extending deadlines, if you frequently feel overburdened or have an excessive workload.

As an illustration, Sarah, a project manager, was overburdened by several projects with conflicting deadlines. She developed the ability to prioritize work according to priority and urgency using efficient time management strategies. Additionally, she understood the need to assign assignments to team members with the required capabilities. By enabling her staff to participate and develop, she could concentrate on activities of high significance that required her skills.

Busy workers may lessen feelings of overload and restore control over their tasks by implementing these time management and prioritizing strategies. By fostering a more harmonious and controllable work-life balance, effective time management increases productivity and promotes mental health.

Having clear limits and expressing defiance guilt-free

We'll talk about how important boundaries are in this part for preserving mental health. We will offer advice on speaking up for yourself and saying no to prevent overcommitting, which can result in more stress and anxiety.

Go through the importance of establishing boundaries to sustain mental health.

Setting limits is essential for preserving mental well-being, particularly for active professionals who frequently deal with conflicting demands and expectations. This is why having limits is crucial:

Preserving one's health: Boundaries ensure that your demands and limitations are respected and safeguard your mental and emotional health. They aid in preventing the weariness, tension, and burnout that might result from overextending oneself.

Promoting a healthy work-life balance: Setting boundaries enables you to commit time and effort to your personal and professional lives. Finding a balance improves general well-being, fortifies bonds, and stops the blurring of boundaries that might result in undue stress from the job.

Increasing attention and productivity: Setting aside time for focused work increases productivity and concentration. You can retain concentration on vital work and reduce unneeded stress by setting boundaries around interruptions and distractions.

Upholding positive bonds with others: Boundaries support wholesome and respectful interactions with coworkers, friends, and family. By being upfront and honest about your wants and limitations, you promote understanding amongst people, improving the caliber of your relationships and minimizing confrontations.

Advice on how to express oneself and refuse requests to avoid taking on too much

The ability to assert oneself and say no are crucial for controlling workload and preserving mental health. Here are some tips for establishing limits and refusing without feeling bad:

Consider your priorities: To lay the groundwork for defining limits, make sure your beliefs, objectives, and priorities are clear. Determine your top priorities, personally and professionally, and set your obligations by them.

Use forceful communication:

1. Communicate your boundaries to people clearly and politely.

2. Describe your restrictions, availability, and preferences regarding workload, due dates, and expectations.

3. Without blaming others, express your wants using "I" expressions.

Develop self-compassion: Accept that prioritizing your well-being is both appropriate and vital. Saying no to some obligations is not a sign of frailty but rather a manifestation of self-care. Don't beat yourself up for having boundaries and saying no; practice self-compassion.

Suggest substitute remedies: If you must deny a request, provide an alternate course of action or propose another source of assistance. Your desire to uphold your limits while assisting others is demonstrated by this.

Control internal speech: Confront any concerns or beliefs that prevent you from setting limits or refusing requests. Remember that setting boundaries benefits you and others in the long run and that your well-being comes first.

For instance, when marketing expert Emily kept accepting new assignments without considering her current workload, she realized the necessity to establish limits. She learned to decline requests that might overburden her schedule by asserting and articulating her boundaries. She felt less stressed out as a consequence, and she could better combine her job and personal life.

Busy professionals may set clear boundaries, safeguard their mental health, and prevent over-committing by using these techniques. It's important to remember that creating boundaries is a continuous process that calls for self-awareness, assertiveness, and self-compassion. It allows you to design a workplace that promotes mental health and encourages personal and professional success.

DEVELOPING COPING MECHANISMS

Acquiring effective coping skills

In this chapter, we will discuss the significance of developing healthy coping skills so that you can properly handle stress and obstacles. We will discuss various coping mechanisms, including journaling, artistic outlets, and exercise, and we will urge readers to develop healthy and positive coping mechanisms to deal with the pressures of their personal and professional life.

Examine coping mechanisms such as journaling, artistic outlets, and exercise.

Coping strategies provide people with the tools to manage stress, maintain their mental health, and build resilience. A few coping mechanisms for professionals who have hectic lives include:

Keep a journal: Encourage readers to keep a diary for emotional expression and self-reflection. Writing down ideas, emotions, and experiences can aid emotional processing, clarity, and stress relief.

Outlets for creativity: Encourage creative things like writing, performing music, painting, sketching, and other crafts. These outlets enable people to manage emotions, lessen stress, and promote happiness and fulfillment.

Physical activity: Stress the value of exercise for maintaining mental health. Regular exercise elevates mood by releasing endorphins, lowering stress hormones, and reducing anxiety. Find physical activities that you love doing and can fit into your hectic schedule, and encourage readers to do the same.

Meditation and mindfulness: Make a point of stressing the advantages of mindfulness and meditation as coping techniques. These techniques encourage tranquility, self-awareness, and the capacity to handle challenges with more resilience and composure.

Motivate readers to develop wholesome coping mechanisms for stress and difficulties.

Because each person is different, something other than what serves as a coping method for one person might not be effective for another. Encourage readers to research and identify coping mechanisms that are personal to them. Remind them to look for positive, healthy methods to deal with stress and difficulties while considering their hobbies, preferences, and requirements.

For instance, Mark, a demanding businessman, found comfort in writing amid his busy schedule. He made it a practice to record his ideas, emotions, and experiences after each day. He became clearer, regulated his tension, and kept his equilibrium thanks to this exercise. Lisa, a lawyer, on the other hand, found that physical activity, particularly yoga, gave her a sense of serenity and stress reduction despite her hectic workload.

Busy professionals may build effective techniques to manage stress and difficulties by investigating and implementing good coping mechanisms, improving their general well-being and resilience.

In the following parts, we will go into more detail on fostering emotional resilience and looking for help to improve people's coping skills and general well-being. These extra techniques can help time-pressed professionals overcome challenges and failures more easily, ensuring that their mental health remains a top priority.

Increasing emotional toughness

This chapter will discuss the idea of emotional resilience and how crucial it is for overcoming professional and personal obstacles. We will discuss how emotional resilience enables people to recover from setbacks and provide useful exercises and ways to cultivate resilience.

Describe emotional resilience and its significance for overcoming obstacles in both personal and professional life.

The term "emotional resilience" refers to the capacity to adjust, deal with, and recover from trying circumstances or adversity. It entails adopting an optimistic outlook, preserving emotional stability, and successfully dealing with obstacles. Why emotional toughness is crucial is as follows:

Overcoming obstacles: People face personal and professional difficulties, setbacks, and barriers. Emotionally resilient individuals can better deal with these difficulties, recover from setbacks, and grow from experiences.

Controlling anxiety and emotions: Resilient People can control their emotions and cope with hardship. They are more capable of handling pressure-filled circumstances, disagreements and maintaining emotional stability in the face of difficulty.

Improving analytical abilities: Through the encouragement of a flexible and proactive mentality, emotional resilience improves problem-solving abilities. Resilient people are more inclined to look for answers, consider difficulties as chances for improvement, and change their strategy when faced with difficulties.

Fostering overall well-being: By encouraging a positive perspective, boosting self-confidence, and developing appropriate coping skills, emotional resilience supports overall well-being. Resilient people are more likely to report higher levels of life satisfaction, keep up good relationships, and feel fulfilled in their work.

Provide useful drills and methods for boosting resiliency and recovering from failures.

Through various activities and strategies, one may assist their path toward developing emotional resilience. Here are some viable tactics for promoting resilience:

Cultivating self-awareness: Exploring readers' talents, values, and emotions might help readers become more self-aware. Through self-reflection, people better comprehend who they are and how they respond to difficulties.

Using optimism and constructive thought: Encourage readers to think positively, frame negative ideas, and develop a positive outlook. Help them identify their inner dialogue and swap out limiting narratives with more empowered ones.

Establishing a network of allies: Promote the value of creating and keeping a solid support network. Encourage readers to ask for assistance from friends, family, mentors, or mental health specialists. Resilience may be strengthened through trying times by exchanging experiences, asking for advice, and getting support.

Practicing problem-solving techniques: Teach readers how to solve problems by breaking them down into manageable parts, creating creative solutions, and considering different angles. Please encourage them to approach issues with a growth perspective and see setbacks as chances for improvement.

Taking care of yourself: Emphasize self-care activities' role in preserving emotional resilience. Encourage readers to take part in relaxation, self-compassion, and stimulating activities. This might involve engaging in mindfulness exercises, hobbies, spending time in nature, or getting help from a professional when necessary.

As an illustration, Sarah, a busy professional, suffered a major setback when her company proposal was turned down. She exercised self-awareness, acknowledged her feelings, and reframed her ideas to put the lessons she had gained from the event in the forefront of her mind as she established emotional resilience. She turned to her mentor for assistance, who gave advice and assisted her in coming up with different action plans. Through these techniques, Sarah could recover, alter her strategy, and ultimately succeed in her career.

By integrating these useful exercises and approaches, busy workers may build emotional resilience and recover quickly from setbacks. Remember that developing resilience is a continuous process that calls for dedication, introspection, and practice. It gives people the skills they need to overcome obstacles with more tenacity and adaptability, thereby improving their general success and well-being.

Seeking assistance and creating a network of allies

The advantages of asking friends, family, or mental health experts for help will be discussed in this chapter. To improve coping skills and general well-being, we will review the value of creating a support system and offer advice on creating meaningful connections.

Discuss the advantages of getting help from friends, family, or mental health specialists.

Finding effective coping methods and preserving mental well-being need seeking help from others. Getting assistance has the following advantages:

Emotional approval: Emotional affirmation comes through talking about our struggles and experiences with encouraging others. It makes us feel less isolated in our challenges and more understood and appreciated. This affirmation fosters warmth and a sense of connection.

Perspective and suggestions: Gaining new thoughts and views is possible while seeking help. We may handle issues more successfully with friends, family, and mental health specialists who can provide direction, fresh perspectives, and advice.

Motivating and inspiring: In trying circumstances, supportive people may provide comfort, inspiration, and encouragement. Their encouragement can motivate us to persist despite difficulty and preserve a positive viewpoint.

Skill-building: Getting help from mental health specialists enables the creation of certain coping mechanisms and plans catering to the person's needs. These experts can offer resources to help you control your emotions, manage stress, and enhance your general well-being.

Advise on creating a network of allies and establishing deep bonds.

Relationships and genuine connections must be fostered to build a support network. Here are some tips for doing it:

Find those who are helpful: Consider the individuals in your life who are encouraging, wise, and sympathetic. Think about the friends, family members, coworkers, or mentors you trust and feel comfortable sharing personal information with.

Make your requirements known: Let individuals you seek help from know what you need and why. Tell them how they can help by listening intently, providing counsel, or just being there.

Promote attentive listening: When someone asks for your help, engage in active listening. Make a space where they may express their views and feelings without fear of repercussions. Until they directly want assistance, only show them empathy and affirmation and refrain from attempting to fix their difficulties.

Take part in mutual assistance: Creating a support system requires cooperation. Be eager to help others and be there for them when they need you. This reciprocity builds connections and promotes a sense of belonging.

Ask for expert assistance as necessary: Never hesitate to contact mental health specialists for help if you feel overwhelmed or need specialized support. According to your unique demands, they may offer professional advice and assistance.

Hannah, a hard-working professional, developed a network of friends, a mentor, and a therapist as examples. For emotional support, she frequently contacted her friends, asked her mentor for advice on work-related problems, and routinely attended therapy sessions to learn effective coping skills. Her general well-being and resiliency were boosted by the various help she received from this support system.

Busy professionals may improve their coping skills and general well-being by actively seeking help and developing a support network. Though maintaining genuine relationships requires work and maintenance, the advantages of having a strong network are immeasurable. Individuals may overcome difficulties, develop resilience, and prosper in both their personal and professional life with the help of supportive connections and professional assistance when they work together as a safety net.

NURTURING WORK-LIFE BALANCE

Being aware of the value of work-life balance

This chapter will discuss the importance of work-life balance and how it affects mental health. We will discuss the drawbacks of work-life imbalance and the advantages of striking a healthy balance for overall pleasure and well-being.

Describe the negative effects of balancing work and personal life improperly.

It may damage one's mental health and general contentment when work precedes personal life. Here are a few detrimental effects of an unbalanced work-life and personal life:

Stress and burnout are rising: Continually putting work above personal obligations can cause chronic stress and burnout. It can drain people emotionally and physically, lowering their productivity and general well-being.

Strained relationships: Ties with family, friends, and loved ones might suffer if personal ties are neglected owing to professional pressures. Feelings of loneliness, alienation, and relationship unhappiness can result from a lack of quality time and emotional availability.

Health problems: An unbalanced work-life balance can lead to several health issues, including immune system deterioration, sleep disturbances, and an increased risk of anxiety and depression. Self-care and healthy living practices can have a detrimental effect on one's physical and emotional well-being.

Decreased job satisfaction: Job satisfaction and contentment might be reduced if you concentrate on work and put your personal life on the back burner. People may need more purpose and interest in their professional activities if they feel balanced and fulfilled in other facets of their lives.

Stress the advantages of work-life balance for psychological well-being and general contentment.

Achieving work-life balance has several advantages for general satisfaction and mental health. Here are a few advantages:

Enhanced well-being and lessened stress: By juggling professional and personal obligations, people better control their stress levels, which enhances their mental and emotional health. It offers chances for rest, renewal, and self-care, all necessary for preserving peak mental well-being.

Enhanced connections: Putting your personal life first builds closer ties with your loved ones, family, and friends. Spending quality time with loved ones strengthens bonds, fosters a sense of community, and offers emotional support, all contributing to overall contentment and well-being.

Enhanced creativity and productivity: Increased productivity and creativity in the workplace are supported by work-life balance. The mental renewal and new views from taking vacations, enjoying leisure time, and pursuing hobbies outside work can improve performance and problem-solving skills.

Improved job satisfaction: Greater job satisfaction results from achieving a work-life balance. Setting limits and making time for personal interests may help people find happiness and a sense of purpose in their life, which benefits their engagement and contentment at work.

Busy professionals may give their mental health and general pleasure more priority by realizing the drawbacks of having an unbalanced work-life and knowing the advantages of attaining it. People may successfully integrate their personal and professional lives and succeed by pursuing a work-life balance.

The following parts will discuss creating meaningful leisure activities and establishing boundaries between work and personal life. With the help of these techniques, busy professionals can achieve work-life balance and take care of their mental health, resulting in a more happy and full existence overall.

Techniques for drawing lines between personal and professional life

This section will include useful advice for setting boundaries and distinguishing between work and personal time. We will discuss the difficulties in setting boundaries and provide remedies to assist busy professionals in achieving work-life balance.

Advise on how to set limits and distinguish between work and personal time.

Maintaining a work-life balance requires setting boundaries between work and personal life. Here are some helpful pointers for creating and upholding these boundaries:

Establish precise work hours: Set clear working hours and let coworkers, clients, and superiors know about them. To guarantee that you have designated personal time, set a start and finish time for your workday.

Establish a dedicated work area: Your workstation should be designated as a section of your house or office. This physical division between work and personal life aids in establishing a psychological barrier. Disconnect mentally from work-related activities when you leave your desk.

Establishing online limits: Limit your time monitoring business emails and texts after hours. Use an app that lets you set particular times to monitor work-related messages or think about disabling notifications. By doing this, you may have uninterrupted personal time without distractions.

Set self-care tasks as a priority: To take care of yourself, set aside time for hobbies, exercise, and quality time with loved ones. Treat these obligations as non-negotiable, just like you would with responsibilities linked to your job. Make sure to prioritize this private time in your calendar and guard it.

Be able to refuse: Set boundaries when accepting more work or activities above your capabilities, and learn to be aggressive. Set priorities for your job and learn to say "no" when required. This makes it possible for you to keep your workload reasonable and avoid taking on too much.

Discuss the difficulties in upholding borders and provide remedies

Setting and upholding limits may be difficult, particularly in stressful professional contexts. Here are some typical issues and responses to assist you in maintaining your boundaries:

Sensing obligation or guilt: Setting limits requires overcoming feelings of responsibility or guilt. Remember that looking after your health enables you to be your best self in all aspects of life. Exercise self-compassion and stress the value of a healthy work-life balance.

Fear of being left behind or missing out: Setting limits might be difficult because of the worry that one would lose out on chances or lag. Remind yourself that equilibrium and well-being are necessary for long-term success. Have faith that setting aside time for yourself will improve your overall performance and satisfaction.

Expectations and work culture: Some workplace environments may prioritize long hours and continual availability. Set explicit expectations for your availability and reaction times with coworkers, superiors, and clients while communicating your limits to them. If required, promote a better work-life balance culture inside your company.

Lack of perceived control: Having a limited amount of control over your work schedule might make setting limits appear challenging. Look at areas where you have influence, like improving your time management or assigning work when it makes sense. Find modest adjustments you can make to increase balance, then expand on them over time.

Keep in mind that setting and upholding limits is a continuous process. It might need to be adjusted and occasionally reevaluated. You may achieve a better work-life balance that improves your mental well-being and general contentment by practicing these techniques and tackling the difficulties.

The necessity of designing meaningful leisure activities will be discussed in the section after this, along with ideas for pastimes and interests that support mental well-being and help maintain a healthy work-life balance.

Making purposeful recreational activities

This section will discuss the value of having a life outside of work and offer ideas for pastimes and interests that encourage mental well-being. Achieving work-life balance depends on motivating readers to enjoy and find fulfilment in their free time.

Inspire readers to take part in extracurricular activities they find enjoyable

Maintaining a healthy work-life balance and enhancing general well-being require participation in activities outside of the workplace. Why it's crucial to motivate readers to engage in leisure activities is as follows:

Stress relief and relaxation: Activities for leisure provide people with a way to unwind and relieve stress. Refuel, relax, and move your attention away from the pressures associated with your job by partaking in activities you like.

Enhancing creativity and personal growth: Hobbies and leisure pursuits encourage creativity and personal development. You can discover new hobbies, pick up new abilities, and broaden your horizons, which promotes fulfilment and self-development.

Improving mental wellness: Positive mental health is promoted by engaging in pleasant activities. It raises mood, lessens signs of stress and anxiety, and improves psychological health in general. Increased life satisfaction and pleasure can be attributed to regular engagement in leisure activities.

Maintaining work-life boundaries: Meaningful pastimes aid in creating a distinct boundary between work and personal life. You may maintain a good balance and stop work from devouring your time and identity by setting aside time for interests outside of work.

Make recommendations for pastimes and interests that encourage mental well-being

Here are some recommendations for pastimes and interests that support mental health and work-life balance:

Physical activities: Take part in activities you love, such as yoga, swimming, running, or walking. Physical exercise benefits your physical health and enhances your mood, reduces stress, and improves mental clarity.

Creative pursuits: Investigate your creative side by painting, writing, playing an instrument, or taking pictures. Self-expression, relaxation, joy and success may be cultivated through artistic endeavors.

Mindfulness and meditation: To promote calmness and inner serenity, try mindfulness and meditation. These exercises help people become more aware of themselves, manage their stress, and feel better overall.

Social connections: You may strengthen your social connections by participating in activities with friends, joining clubs or groups with similar interests, or volunteering. A sense of community, support, and pleasure may be found via social connections.

Nature-related activities: Spend time outdoors, whether hiking, gardening, or just taking in the scenery. It has been demonstrated that spending time in nature may lower stress, elevate mood, and improve general well-being.

Learning and personal development: You may explore topics that interest you by enrolling in classes, reading books, or listening to podcasts. Constant learning fosters mental stimulation, individual development, and a sense of success.

Encourage readers to consider their hobbies and interests and prioritize pursuits that make them happy and fulfilled. Remind them that leisure activities shouldn't seem like extra duties but should be selected based on personal preferences. The secret is participating in leisurely pursuits that provide a sense of accomplishment, enabling a full and rewarding life away from work.

In the book's concluding part, we will highlight the most important tactics and lessons learned for obtaining and sustaining mental well-being as a busy professional.

ENHANCING PRODUCTIVITY AND FOCUS

Focus and concentration-boosting methods

This chapter will look at ways to improve attention and concentration because they are so important for mental health and productivity. We'll talk about how distractions affect mental health and productivity and provide useful methods for increasing attention.

Examine how distractions affect both productivity and mental health.

Distractions may seriously reduce productivity and add to feelings of stress and exhaustion. Effective distraction management requires an understanding of their effects. Here's why they're important:

Reduced productivity: The process might be disrupted by constant interruptions and diversions, which can lower output and raise the risk of mistakes. Each distraction results in a pause as you try to restore momentum and attention, which reduces productivity.

Increased stress and overwhelm: Distractions that happen frequently might make you feel stressed and overwhelmed. People who frequently move between jobs and feel like they are being pushed in many different ways may find it difficult to focus and feel mentally exhausted.

Impaired decision-making and creativity: Distractions can impede the ability to think creatively and affect decision-making. Engaging in serious thought and problem-solving becomes easier when attention is frequently distracted, which lowers the caliber of work done.

Discuss ways to sharpen attention, such as time blocking, reducing interruptions, and engaging in serious work

Adopting methods and strategies that reduce interruptions and foster a focused environment are necessary for increasing focus. The following are some methods to sharpen focus:

Time-blocking: Inspire readers to set aside particular time slots for concentrated work. This entails blocking time to focus only on critical work while avoiding interruptions.

Minimizing interruptions: Advise how to reduce interruptions from outside sources, such as turning off notifications, creating limits with coworkers, and designating certain "quiet hours" for concentrated work. Encourage readers to choose a workspace that facilitates focus.

Practicing deep work: Describe deep work, devoting uninterrupted, focused time to significant activities requiring strong concentration. Suggest time management strategies like the Pomodoro Technique, which divides work into concentrated segments and is followed by brief rest periods.

Mindful task-switching: Encourage readers to switch between tasks mindfully when interruptions are unavoidable. People may focus again more quickly by intentionally switching between tasks and spending less time engaging in distractions.

Providing an environment conducive to work: Emphasize the need for a physical setting that encourages concentration. Organizing workplaces, clearing clutter, and using equipment like noise-cancelling headphones or relaxing background music all help.

For instance, a busy professional, Sarah battled recurrent interruptions and diversions throughout her job. She began practicing time-blocking strategies and set aside uninterrupted time for concentrated work. Sarah found that her attention and productivity significantly increased after establishing clear limits with her coworkers, disabling alerts, and setting up a distraction-free workspace.

Busy workers may increase their attention and productivity by being aware of the effects of distractions and putting them into practice. These techniques increase people's sense of achievement, lower their stress levels, and improve their work performance.

The next parts will cover more distraction management techniques, how to develop goals to maximize productivity and a summary of the most important lessons for working professionals who want to attain mental wellness and succeed in their demanding professional life.

Distraction-control techniques

In this part, we'll look at distraction-management techniques for the workplace. We'll discuss typical distractions, suggest solutions for them, and offer advice on how to set up a focused, distraction-free workspace.

Identify typical distractions that occur in the workplace and suggest solutions for each one.

In a professional situation, distractions can come from internal and external difficulties. Recognizing these distractions and creating plans of attack to combat them is crucial. The following list of typical distractions is followed by management advice:

Digital distractions: Online platforms and digital gadgets may be significant sources of distraction. Reduce the amount of time you spend on social media, turn off alerts that aren't necessary, and utilize productivity tools like browser extensions that block or restrict access to websites that are likely to cause distractions.

Interruptions from colleagues: Workflow and attention might be affected by frequent interruptions from coworkers. Set clear limits, politely express your desire for uninterrupted work time, and provide cues to let others know you're working intently by using headphones, for example.

Email overload: The stress of having a full inbox might cause you to neglect critical chores. Put into practice email management techniques include:

- Scheduling certain times to read and react to emails.

- Using filters and folders to organize messages.

- Unsubscribing from pointless email subscriptions.

Meetings and unnecessary interruptions: Meetings frequently cause diversions from important duties and might consume a considerable chunk of the workday. Determine whether meetings are necessary, and strive for effective, focused meetings with precise agendas and time constraints. Meetings that are optional to your job may be declined or rescheduled.

Procrastination and time-wasting activities: Time may be lost via procrastination, and time can be lost through indulging in useless activities. To develop self-discipline, create projects with clear objectives and deadlines, divide them into smaller, more manageable chunks, and use productivity tricks like the "two-minute rule" or the "5-second rule" to fight lethargy.

Offer advice for establishing a focused and distraction-free workplace.

Productivity depends on setting up a workspace that encourages attention and reduces distractions. To create a distraction-free environment, consider the following advice:

Designate a dedicated workspace: Make a designated spot for your workstation, preferably away from private spaces like your bedroom or living room. This physical division aids in establishing a mental wall between work and personal life.

Eliminate visual clutter: As a crowded atmosphere can lead to mental distraction, clear your desk of all superfluous stuff. Just keep necessities around and arrange your physical area to encourage a sense of calm and attention.

Optimize lighting and sound: To suit your tastes, adjust the lights to a suitable level. Reduce noise distractions by using noise-cancelling headphones, listening to background music or white noise, or, if feasible, working in a quiet area.

Establish boundaries with others: Inform individuals around you of your desire for a distraction-free atmosphere. Establish firm boundaries with relatives, roommates, or coworkers to reduce interruptions and distractions during focused work time.

Utilize productivity tools: Use applications and productivity tools that can improve your attention and help you manage distractions. Website blockers, attention clocks, task management applications, and note-taking tools are a few examples of these tools.

Busy workers may maximize their productivity and preserve mental well-being by recognizing frequent distractions, putting techniques to control them into place, and establishing a focused and distraction-free work environment. These techniques make increased focus, efficiency, and a higher sense of success possible.

The book's final section will offer readers advice on setting goals that will maximize productivity, highlight the most important points, and give a thorough overview of all the techniques covered to help busy professionals succeed in their demanding environment while achieving and sustaining mental wellness.

Increasing output through wise goal-setting

This part examines how creating smart goals may help you work more productively. We will advise how to create SMART goals (Specific, Measurable, Achievable, Relevant, Time-Bound) and provide methods for breaking down ambitious objectives into more doable tasks.

Teach readers how to develop SMART objectives.

A tried-and-true method for successful goal-setting is to develop SMART objectives. It offers direction, organization, and a clear road map for reaching goals. To set SMART objectives, follow these steps:

Specific: Encourage readers to create clear and well-defined goals that are detailed. Developing an action plan and tracking results is simpler when the goal is clearer. For instance, instead of establishing a general aim like "improve time management," a more precise target may be "reduce time spent on non-essential tasks by 30%."

Measurable: Identify quantifiable objectives for readers that can be monitored and assessed. Measurable objectives help people stay focused by offering concrete proof of their progress. A quantifiable objective can be to, for instance, "increase monthly sales by 10%" or "complete three client projects per week."

Achievable: Encourage readers to make difficult-yet-achievable objectives. Too simple of a goal could not inspire you enough, while too ambitious of a goal can be too much to handle. Striking a balance and establishing challenging but attainable objectives that can be attained with hard work and devotion is crucial.

Relevant: Encourage readers to develop objectives pertinent to and consistent with their beliefs, priorities, and aspirations in the workplace. Goals that are meaningful and create a sense of purpose are relevant. People are more likely to remain dedicated and motivated when goals reflect their beliefs and interests.

Time-bound: Insist on the value of establishing deadlines or target dates for goals. Setting deadlines for goals makes people feel more accountable and in the moment. Encourage readers to create milestones and break long-term goals into more manageable periods.

Provide techniques for breaking down big objectives into more achievable jobs

One of the most effective methods for raising productivity is to divide larger goals into more manageable, smaller tasks. The following techniques will assist readers in properly breaking down their goals:

Start with the end in mind: Encourage readers to visualize the results they want from their aims. By understanding the end goal, they may work backwards and determine the precise actions required to attain the goal.

Divide and conquer: Help readers by directing them to divide their goals into manageable activities. The objectives are therefore made more manageable and less intimidating. Each activity should be doable and have a specific objective that advances the overall aim.

Prioritize and sequence tasks: Help readers order their to-do lists according to priority and urgency. Determine the essential activities that will most influence goal achievement and focus on them first. Task sequencing makes it possible to advance logically and assures effective use of time and resources.

Set deadlines for tasks: Readers are urged to give each job a due date. A timetable may help with time management and keep people on track by instilling a feeling of urgency and order.

Celebrate milestones: Remind readers to recognize and appreciate their accomplishments as they go along. By motivating people and giving them a sense of success, milestone recognition increases dedication and productivity.

For instance, if a busy professional wants to create a new marketing campaign, breaking it down into smaller jobs may entail doing market research, coming up with creative ideas, creating images, and putting the plan into action. The professional can achieve their bigger aim by concentrating on these doable tasks and moving forward steadily.

The productivity of busy professionals can be increased by defining SMART objectives and breaking them down into smaller tasks. This method offers precision, focus, and a well-thought-out strategy for reaching goals. It gives people the ability to maintain concentration, monitor their progress, and take little steps in the direction of their objectives.

In the last part, we will provide a thorough summary of the book's content and recommendations by summarizing the essential tactics and lessons for obtaining and sustaining mental well-being as a busy professional.

CULTIVATING POSITIVE MENTAL HEALTH HABITS

Including self-care routines in everyday activities

This chapter will discuss the value of self-care in preserving mental well-being and offer a variety of self-care techniques that may quickly fit into a working professional's hectic schedule.

Go through the significance of self-care for preserving mental health.

A crucial component of preserving mental well-being is self-care. It entails consciously attending to physiological, psychological, and emotional needs. Why self-care is so important for working professionals is as follows:

Stress reduction: Self-care activities help you feel less stressed. It enables people to refuel and refill their energies, fostering serenity and equilibrium.

Enhancing overall well-being: Self-care routines help to increase general well-being. Making time for oneself improves resilience, lifts mood, raises self-esteem and prevents burnout.

Increased productivity: Making self-care a priority improves productivity. People may sharpen their attention, enhance their cognitive capacities, and develop problem-solving techniques by planning activities that revitalize and nourish the mind and body.

Role modelling: Self-care provides a good example for friends, family, and coworkers. Busy workers foster a culture of mental well-being by prioritizing self-care and encouraging others to do the same.

Offer a variety of self-care techniques that a busy professional may readily fit into their calendar.

It's crucial to provide self-care techniques that working professionals may easily use. Listed below are a few simple self-care techniques that may be implemented into a daily schedule:

Physical self-care: Encourage frequent activity, even if it's only a brief stretch during a break or a fast stroll. For optimum physical and mental health, priorities nourishing meals, proper fluids, and adequate sleep.

Emotional self-care: Take part in activities that enhance emotional well-being, such as journaling, mindfulness or meditation training, or, if necessary, therapy or counselling. Give yourself time to think and express yourself.

Social self-care: Develop enduring relationships with family, friends, coworkers, or networks in your career. Plan time for social activities, such as having coffee with friends or engaging in shared interests or hobbies.

Intellectual self-care: Read novels, listen to instructional podcasts, or participate in mentally demanding activities to stimulate the mind. Allocate time for your development and to pursue your interests in learning.

Relaxation and leisure: Spend time relaxing and indulging in enjoyable activities that help you decompress, such as taking baths, participating in hobbies, listening to music, or pursuing creative endeavors.

For instance, a busy professional like Sarah incorporates self-care into her daily routine by getting up 15 minutes earlier to practice mindfulness and allocating time in the afternoons for leisure reading. These simple yet deliberate actions significantly improve her mental health.

Busy workers may include self-care into their daily routines to improve their mental and general well-being by highlighting its significance and offering a variety of practical activities.

The power of appreciation and optimism and techniques for creating resilience and adjusting to change in the workplace will all be discussed in the parts that follow as essential elements of developing good mental health practices.

Using the strength of thankfulness and optimism

This chapter will examine the effects of thankfulness and optimistic thinking on mental health. We will discuss the benefits of a positive outlook on life and provide activities and methods to help people be more grateful and optimistic daily.

Examine how thankfulness and optimistic thinking might improve mental health.

Positive thinking and feelings of gratitude have a significant influence on mental health. Why they are crucial for working professionals is explained here:

Improved well-being and mood: Gratitude and optimistic thinking exercises can improve mood and well-being in general. People develop a sense of happiness and contentment by praising what they have and finding the good things in life.

Decreased anxiety and stress: Stress and anxiety levels can be lowered by practicing gratitude and positive thinking. Worries can be reduced, and a better sense of calm can be fostered by focusing on what is going well and adopting a positive outlook.

Increased resiliency: Having an optimistic outlook helps people be more resilient, which helps them deal with obstacles and failures more successfully. Thinking positively encourages problem-solving talents, flexibility, and confidence in one's capacity to overcome challenges.

Enhanced connections: Gratitude exercises strengthen and deepen interpersonal relationships. Thankfulness builds bridges, fosters empathy, and fosters a pleasant and encouraging environment among coworkers, friends, and loved ones.

Provide practical activities and methods for developing a positive outlook.

Positive attitude development takes deliberate effort and repetition. Here are some useful activities and methods to encourage appreciation and optimism among busy professionals:

Journaling your gratitude: Encourage readers to create a thankfulness diary and list three daily things they are thankful for. This routine encourages appreciation for the good things in life and moves the emphasis there.

Positive statements: Encourage readers to create and consistently repeat positive affirmations. Positive phrases known as affirmations serve to boost optimism and self-belief. Write affirmations about your professional objectives or personal qualities. Encourage readers to do the same.

Kind deeds: Encourage others to show kindness to one another by helping out, complimenting, or expressing their thanks. Performing acts of kindness benefits those who receive them and enhances one's well-being and optimism.

Meditation on gratitude: Encourage readers to cultivate mindful thankfulness by taking daily breaks to appreciate things intentionally. This might be as easy as slowing down to enjoy a cup of coffee or going for a stroll to take in the sights of nature.

Changing unfavorable perceptions: Teach readers to recognize unfavorable thought patterns and to reframe them in favor of the positive. People may develop a positive attitude by confronting negative self-talk and substituting it with more uplifting and powerful ideas.

As an illustration, Sarah keeps a gratitude notebook and expresses her thanks for the assistance and successes of her coworkers. She also includes positive affirmations in her daily routine to stay motivated and have a good mindset.

Busy workers may create a good mentality that improves their mental well-being and general contentment by learning about the advantages of gratitude and positive thinking and providing them with useful exercises and practices.

As essential elements of developing excellent mental health habits for busy professionals, we will concentrate on resilience and adaptation in the professional context in the following section.

Developing resiliency and flexibility

This chapter will examine the function of resilience in preserving mental health in the face of adversity. We will discuss why building resilience is crucial for navigating the working world and offer techniques for promoting resilience and changing with the times.

Describe how resilience plays a role in preserving mental well-being in the face of adversity.

Being resilient means recovering from setbacks, adjusting to change, and sustaining happiness in the face of difficulty. It is essential for preserving mental health through trying circumstances. Here are some reasons why busy professionals should practice resilience:

Stress reduction: People with resilience are better able to control their stress. It helps individuals handle demanding circumstances, recover from failures, and maintain their composure and control.

Ability to adapt to change: People with resilience can adjust to changes in the workplace. Being able to successfully handle changes, accept new challenges, and grab opportunities is essential in today's fast-paced and dynamic work contexts.

Positive attitude: Resilient people view failures as transitory obstacles that can be learned from. It encourages positivity, tenacity, and confidence in one's capacity to go beyond challenges.

Optimal mental health: Resilience development improves general mental health. It aids people in developing the emotional steadiness, self-assurance, and sense of purpose necessary to thrive in difficult work contexts.

Advise on how to become resilient and adjust to change in the workplace.

The adoption of specific methods and deliberate effort are needed to develop resilience. The following are some methods for promoting resilience and adjusting to change in the workplace:

Develop a growth attitude: Encourage readers to adopt a growth mindset, emphasizing ongoing learning, accepting difficulties, and viewing setbacks as chances for improvement. This thinking enables people to change, grow from failures, and learn new things.

Create a network of allies: Insist on having a network of friends, mentors, or coworkers who can offer support, inspiration, and perspective during trying times. A robust support network boosts resilience and aids people in navigating challenges.

Engage in self-care: Stress the role that self-care plays in promoting resilience. Encourage readers to prioritize healthy lifestyle choices, such as getting enough sleep, exercising, eating a balanced diet, and participating in enjoyable activities.

Hone your problem-solving abilities: Improve readers' problem-solving abilities, which is crucial for overcoming challenges and adjusting to change. Teach techniques include:

- Looking for alternate solutions.
- Breaking down complicated problems into smaller, achievable tasks.
- Getting feedback from others as necessary.

Encourage flexibility: Encourage a flexible and adaptable way of thinking. Stress the value of accepting change, being receptive to fresh perspectives, and constantly looking for chances to learn and develop.

For instance, when faced with a significant organizational shift, Sarah proactively asked her dependable coworkers and mentors for help. She also engaged in regular exercise and mindfulness practices as forms of self-care. These techniques assisted her in handling the transition effectively and preserving her mental health.

Busy professionals may flourish in demanding work situations, overcome difficulties, and preserve their general well-being by recognizing the importance of resilience in preserving mental wellness and implementing tactics for developing resilience and adjusting to change.

To help busy professionals on their path to obtaining and sustaining mental well-being in a demanding environment, we will present a complete review of the important methods and practices covered throughout the book in the concluding portion.

SEEKING PROFESSIONAL HELP WHEN NEEDED

Recognizing the symptoms that may indicate the need for professional assistance

The significance of identifying the warning indications that seeking professional assistance for mental health may be essential will be covered in this chapter. We will inform readers of the warning signals of more severe mental health issues and stress the significance of getting care immediately if symptoms intensify or continue.

Inform readers about symptoms of more severe mental health issues

People must be aware of the symptoms that need seeking expert assistance. While stress and depression are prevalent, some signs may point to more severe mental health issues. We can aid readers in understanding their mental health by educating them on these symptoms. Some warning indications are as follows:

a. Prolonged emotions of melancholy, hopelessness, or despair that are overpowering and persistent.
b. Severe anxiety or panic episodes that disrupt normal daily activities.
c. Unintentional changes in appetite or weight, such as substantial weight loss or increase.
d. Sleep issues that affect everyday living, such as insomnia, nightmares, or extreme drowsiness.
e. Decision-making or concentration issues that cause issues at work or in personal relationships.
f. Loss of enjoyment or interest in once-enjoyed activities; this shows a lack of drive or zeal.
g. Constantly having suicidal or death thoughts or injuring oneself.

h.   Social retreat and separation from loved ones or friends.
i.   A rise in drug misuse or dependence on harmful coping strategies.
j.   Physical problems that are unexplained, such as headaches, stomachaches, or persistent discomfort.

Encourage patients to seek medical attention when symptoms intensify or persist.

It is crucial to stress that asking for professional assistance is a proactive move toward improved mental health. Encourage readers to consider their symptoms' timeframe, severity, and effects. It is crucial to get expert help if symptoms last or worsen over time. Let readers know that asking for assistance shows strength and self-care.

Describe how mental health specialists with the proper training, such as therapists, psychologists, psychiatrists, or counsellors, may offer the required assistance and direction. They can evaluate symptoms, diagnose mental health, and provide suitable treatments. Educate readers about the benefits of early intervention and therapy for better outcomes and overall wellbeing.

We provide readers with the tools they need to take charge of their mental health and get the care they require by identifying the warning signals that seeking professional help may be necessary and encouraging people to do so when symptoms continue or get worse.

In the following parts, we'll give an overview of mental health resources and assistance and talk about how encouraging talks about mental health may help everyone feel supported.

Overview of available tools and services for mental health

We will give an overview of the mental health resources and support services accessible to anyone seeking professional assistance in this chapter. We will highlight the significance of de-stigmatizing mental health concerns and getting treatment without feeling ashamed while also providing information about therapists, counsellors, and support groups.

Describe the resources for mental health that are out there, such as therapists, counsellors, and support groups.

It's crucial to tell readers about the support networks and services for mental health that are accessible to them. This may consist of:

Counsellors and therapists: Give information about qualified therapists, psychologists, psychiatrists, or counsellors who have a range of mental health specialties. Help readers pick a practitioner that best meets their requirements by outlining the various therapeutic philosophies.

Group therapy: Discuss the existence of support groups, both offline and online, where people may get in touch with others who have had similar experiences. Give details about support groups concentrating on specific mental health issues or overall well-being.

Hotlines and assistance lines: Share the phone numbers of hotlines or helplines that provide 24/7 support to anyone needing emotional support or instant assistance. These programs can offer support, direction, and recommendations to the right resources.

Stress the value of de-stigmatizing mental health concerns and getting guilt-free assistance.

Addressing the stigma associated with mental health is essential to enable people to seek treatment without feeling guilty or afraid of being judged. We may assist in removing obstacles and creating an environment that is more encouraging by talking about the following topics:

Normalize seeking assistance: Insist that getting assistance for mental health issues is just as vital as getting assistance for physical diseases. A proactive step towards better mental health is to seek professional help. Mental health is a crucial component of total well-being.

Inform people about mental health: Describe the prevalence of prevalent mental health issues and the results of receiving professional treatment. Help readers realize that anybody may have mental health problems and that getting help shows courage and self-care.

Encourage candid dialogue: Encourage candid and open discussions about mental health to lessen stigma. To offer a secure environment for people to share their experiences, encourage readers to do the same. Encourage support, compassion, and empathy for people who are seeking assistance.

Promote the available resources: Promote the accessibility of resources and support networks for mental health. Encourage readers to notify their networks about services, helping to further de-stigmatize obtaining professional assistance.

We can promote better mental health and well-being by educating people about mental health services, emphasizing the need to de-stigmatize mental health conditions, and encouraging people to seek treatment without feeling guilty.

To help busy professionals on their path to obtaining and sustaining mental well-being in a demanding environment, we will present a complete review of the important methods and practices covered throughout the book in the concluding portion.

Promoting dialogues about mental health that are stigma-free

In this chapter, we will stress the value of promoting talks about mental health that are free of stigma. We will promote open communication on mental well-being in the workplace and interpersonal relationships and provide advice on starting and participating in such talks.

Support open communication about mental health in the workplace and interpersonal interactions

Establishing a culture that values open communication about mental health in both professional and interpersonal settings is critical. Here's why it's crucial:

Workplace: Encourage leaders and companies to foster a supportive work environment and raise awareness of mental health issues. Encourage businesses to offer services, including mental health initiatives, employee support programs, and training on mental health awareness. Encourage an environment where workers may speak openly about their mental health issues without being afraid of being judged or suffering repercussions.

Personal connections: Stress the need to sustain supportive connections for mental well-being. Encourage your loved ones to create a welcoming environment where people can discuss their mental health without feeling judged. Help people realize that asking for help from their support network is not a sign of weakness but rather a proactive move toward well-being.

Provide instructions on starting and participating in constructive dialogues regarding mental well-being.

Empathy, compassion, and attentive listening are necessary for starting and participating in helpful dialogues regarding mental well-being. Give instructions on how to establish a place free from stigma:

Display compassion and empathy: People should be urged to approach discussions about mental health with compassion and sensitivity. Validate the experiences and feelings of the other person by demonstrating your comprehension of them. As a result, a secure and accepting environment is created for sharing.

Listening attentively: Explain the value of active listening to the reader. Please encourage them to pay attentively intently, refrain from interjecting, and reply in a sympathetic and understanding manner. People who actively listen feel heard and cherished.

Use empathetic language: Encourage people to talk about mental health in a friendly and nonjudgmental manner. Encourage people to avoid forming assumptions or making snap judgments. Instead, concentrate on providing assistance, inspiration, and comprehension.

Describe your own experiences: When appropriate, please encourage others to talk about their personal experiences with mental health. They may lessen the stigma associated with mental health by being honest about their problems and personal development, and they can encourage others to follow suit.

For instance, Sarah starts discussions on mental health at team meetings, fostering a supportive work environment. She invites guest speakers, distributes information, and promotes open communication among coworkers about their well-being. Consequently, the team is at ease asking for help and using resources for their mental health.

We can help lessen the stigma associated with mental health and promote a more supportive and understanding society by advocating for open communication about mental health in the workplace and personal relationships and by providing advice on starting and participating in supportive conversations about mental wellness.

To help busy professionals on their path to obtaining and sustaining mental well-being in a demanding environment, we will present a complete review of the important methods and practices covered throughout the book in the concluding portion.

SUSTAINING MENTAL WELLNESS IN THE LONG TERM

Developing a long-term strategy for mental well-being

This chapter advises readers on creating a tailored long-term mental wellness maintenance strategy. We will advise on developing objectives and implementing plans promoting continued mental health.

Assist readers in creating an individual strategy for preserving mental well-being.

Ensure the readers know the significance of developing a long-term mental wellness strategy. This strategy will act as a road map for preserving mental health throughout time. Give readers the following instructions so they may create their unique plan:

Consider present procedures: Encourage readers to consider the methods and strategies that have been most effective for them so far in achieving mental well-being. Their long-term plan will be built based on this self-reflection.

Identify the main areas of interest: Help readers determine the essential components of their mental health that they wish to give top priority in the long run. These are a few examples of self-care, stress management, interpersonal connections, professional fulfilment, and personal growth.

Set precise objectives: Help readers develop SMART goals—specific, measurable, realistic, relevant, and time-bound—for their mental health. These objectives should complement their primary areas of attention and offer a precise course for their continuing work.

Create a plan of action: Assist readers in dividing their objectives into manageable steps. These actions should be doable and practicable, given their daily schedules and obligations. Encourage readers to have reasonable expectations and to be adaptable enough to change their course of action as necessary.

Offer advice on developing long-term objectives and putting them into practice.

Advise on how to use tactics for long-term mental well-being and develop significant goals:

Accountability and consistency: Stress the value of being consistent when putting mental wellness techniques into practice. Encourage readers to develop routines and habits to help them achieve their objectives. Also, recommend accountability practices like keeping track of progress, getting help from a reliable person, or joining a support group.

regular self-evaluation: Encourage readers to periodically evaluate their mental health and revise their tactics as necessary. They can keep aware of their shifting requirements and make the required adjustments to their strategy with the aid of self-reflection and review.

Adaptability and flexibility: Remind readers that situations can change since life is dynamic. Please encourage them to be adaptable and change their strategy as needed. To do this, you should be willing to experiment with new ideas, consider several avenues, and request further assistance as necessary.

Overcoming challenges and keeping up motivation

In this part, we'll discuss typical challenges people may encounter when attempting to maintain their mental well-being and offer solutions. Maintaining long-term mental health requires identifying and successfully overcoming these challenges.

Identify typical barriers to sustaining mental well-being and provide solutions for them

Time restrictions and work pressures: Professionals who lead busy lives sometimes deal with time limits and responsibilities connected to their jobs, making prioritizing their mental health difficult. To go over this difficulty:

Management of time: Encourage people to prioritize and set aside time for activities that promote mental well-being. Assist them in determining time-wasting activities that may be reduced or abandoned to make room for self-care.

Boundaries: Stress the value of creating boundaries between your personal and professional lives. Encourage people to set up boundaries by disabling work alerts during personal time, limiting the number of hours they may work, and, where practical, delegating duties.

Outside stressors: Many external stressors in life include obligations to one's family, financial strains, and unforeseen catastrophes. To go over this difficulty:

Stress reduction methods: Offer a variety of stress-reduction methods, including deep breathing exercises, meditation, and physical activity. Please encourage them to find strategies that suit them best and incorporate them into their everyday routines.

Auxiliary system: Encourage people to use their support network when they need assistance. Guidance, a sympathetic ear, and useful assistance can be obtained from friends, family, or mental health specialists.

Insufficient drive or complacency: Sometimes people may need help staying motivated or developing a complacent attitude. To go over this difficulty:

Goal reevaluation: Assist people in reevaluating their objectives to ensure they mesh with their current priorities and values. This may include frequently reviewing and changing their goals to keep a sense of purpose and drive.

Accountability: To keep motivated, advise joining a support group or finding an accountability partner. People may maintain their goals by checking in frequently, discussing their progress, and getting support from others.

Honor accomplishments: Please encourage others to recognize and appreciate all of their accomplishments. Acknowledge and praise progress to keep motivation high and foster a positive outlook.

Self-care is not prioritized: Due to conflicting expectations and duties, many people need help setting aside time for their needs. To go over this difficulty:

Mindset change: Help people understand the importance of self-care to their general well-being and productivity. Please encourage them to see self-care as an investment in themselves instead of indulgent behaviors.

Begin modestly: Encourage people to begin with simple self-care routines that they may readily incorporate into their daily schedules. This might involve participating in enjoyable activities, taking quick pauses, or practicing mindfulness.

Adjustment and reflection: Encourage people to review their self-care routines frequently and tweak them as necessary. This may include experimenting with various tactics or obtaining expert advice to figure out what works best for them.

By addressing frequent roadblocks and providing solutions, people may build resilience and learn how to negotiate difficulties while preserving mental well-being successfully. These methods will support people in maintaining their self-care routines even in the face of difficulties or disappointments.

To help busy professionals on their path to obtaining and sustaining mental well-being in a demanding environment, we will present a complete review of the important methods and practices covered throughout the book in the concluding portion.

Supporting personal development and lifelong learning

The significance of continual personal development and self-improvement in sustaining mental well-being will be emphasized in this section. We will recommend books, podcasts, seminars, and courses connected to mental well-being and urge readers to adopt a philosophy of lifelong learning.

Promote continuing self-improvement and personal development to maintain mental well-being

Mindset for lifelong learning: Insist on the value of developing an attitude of ongoing personal development and progress. Encourage readers to think of life as an adventure of learning and development, with every encounter providing a chance for growth and self-discovery.

Practices for personal development: Encourage participating in personal development tasks like journaling, reflection exercises, or self-evaluation tools. These methods promote personal development and well-being by assisting people in understanding their values, strengths, and areas for development.

fostering curiosity: Encourage readers to pursue new experiences and information by fostering their curiosity. This might be learning new things, experimenting with different pastimes, or pursuing pursuits that cognitively stimulate and challenge them.

List books, podcasts, workshops, or training courses relevant to mental well-being.

Books: Provide a carefully chosen collection of books on diverse subjects relevant to mental health, personal development, and self-improvement. Include literature on emotional intelligence, positive psychology, stress management, mindfulness, and resilience. Give succinct descriptions of each book to assist readers in selecting ones that match their interests.

Podcasts: Give podcast recommendations with an emphasis on mental health, overall health, and personal growth. These podcasts can offer insightful commentary, professional interviews, and useful advice promoting mental well-being. Podcasts covering mindfulness, self-care, a good outlook, and personal development techniques should be included.

Classes or workshops: Inform people about personal development or mental health seminars, or online courses. These sites can provide those looking to improve their well-being with organized learning opportunities and useful tools. Include details about reliable websites or businesses that provide these materials.

People may increase their awareness of mental well-being and learn skills and techniques for long-term well-being maintenance by fostering ongoing personal development and self-improvement.

To help busy professionals on their path to obtaining and sustaining mental well-being in a demanding environment, we will present a complete review of the important methods and practices covered throughout the book in the concluding portion.

The main methods for achieving mental wellness covered throughout the book will be summarized in this final chapter. We will also express our belief in the readers' capacity to succeed in a demanding society and offer closing remarks on the transformative effects of prioritizing mental wellness in the workplace.

A summary of the most effective methods for improving mental well-being

We will briefly summarize the main ideas covered in each chapter in this part, reminding readers of the important skills they have developed on their path to mental wellness. This summary will act as a reminder and point of reference for readers to review and solidify their comprehension of the techniques.

Demonstrate faith in the readers' capacity to succeed in a challenging environment.

We shall exhibit faith in the readers' capacity to live successfully and manage a complex world while putting their mental health first. Please encourage them to recognize their advancements and their tenacity and resolve in putting the book's recommendations into practice. Let readers know they have a solid foundation and a wide range of tools for preserving their mental well-being.

Concluding remarks on the transformational potential of making mental well-being a priority in a professional setting

In this part, we'll offer some closing remarks on the positive impact of emphasizing mental well-being in the workplace. Emphasize the beneficial effects of spending money on mental well-being in a professional's life, including productivity, work happiness, and general well-being.

Stress the value of viewing mental wellness as a journey rather than a final goal. Encourage readers to keep pursuing improvement, experimenting with and putting new ideas into practice as they pursue mental well-being.

Give instances or tales of people who have made mental well-being a top priority and have seen a big improvement in their careers. These experiences will motivate and reaffirm the idea that putting mental well-being first is a good goal with real rewards.

Encourage readers to remain dedicated to their pursuit of mental well-being, to seek help when necessary, and to modify their plans as needs change. Remind them that their mental health comes first and that they are entitled to success in their personal and professional lives.

Finally, thank the readers for taking the time and making an effort to improve their mental health. Reiterate the value of prioritizing mental health in a demanding world and reassure them that by using the techniques they have learned to attain and maintain mental well-being while succeeding in their career goals.

The book will leave readers feeling empowered, motivated, and prepared to start their journey towards a fulfilling and balanced life by offering a thorough conclusion summarizing the key strategies, affirming confidence in the readers' abilities, and highlighting the transformative power of prioritizing mental wellness.

This marks the end of the book "How to Achieve Mental Wellness: Strategies for Busy Professionals Thriving in a Demanding World." This book's readers find it a useful tool and guidance as they confront the possibilities and difficulties that lie ahead. Remember that your mental health matters and that you may live a life of meaning, resiliency, and success by giving it priority.

www.ingramcontent.com/pod-product-compliance
Lightning Source LLC
Chambersburg PA
CBHW061004260726

48661CB00005B/2051